Collection of Poems

Time
~ *Has* ~
Come!

Mwepu Kalenga

authorHOUSE®

AuthorHouse™
1663 Liberty Drive
Bloomington, IN 47403
www.authorhouse.com
Phone: 1 (800) 839-8640

Published by AuthorHouse   03/31/2015

ISBN: 978-1-4969-7492-1 (sc)
ISBN: 978-1-4969-7490-7 (e)

Library of Congress Control Number: 2015903865

Print information available on the last page.

Contents

Where are you eagle youth,
Ignoring the truth,
Praising the tiny
For a penny?

You resemble that slave   5
Though brave
Who denied release
But has never been at ease.

During the 60's Achebe awoke
Through his work   10
His youth
Whereby the truth.

But you are still still
As if in a hill
Wherein illnesses   15
Are but weaknesses.

Is it that long way
Foreseen in Chinua Achebe's play,
Undergone by his disciples
That you grant as principles?   20

Do recover your identity
By expressing your ability
To reconcile traditionalism
To postmodernism.

Save your Africa   25
From South-Africa
Through Congo
ToTogo…

To you I dedicate these lyrics!!!

Acknowledgment

It behooves me to express my profound gratitude to all those great figures who put their blessing hands, knowledge, time, prayers and feelings for the realization of this collection of poems. Frankly without their hands this would remain virtual as most of human's useful dreams.

It gives me more than a pleasure to acknowledge the natural love and respect that I have been an eternal beneficiary from my parents. May you be dead to my eyes, Mulopwe Luvula Kyasha, you always cherish my heart and my wit. I am always double indebted to your tender wife, Kayumba Musense for her permanent encouragement as if she was an old scholar.

I am deeply indebted to my children Mwape Kibwela, Kalenga Kalebanya, Nteta Kamponge and Mwepu Kalenga Masanza for their true companionship and comprehension. They have been enduring from my double absence home. Therefore, their interruptions for curious questions about what I was writing about everyday – that indeed they were fed up with- helped me to realize that I was finally a father.

To their tender mother, my wife and permanent companion Katondo Kalenga, I miss the word for she has accepted heartedly to share the best and the worst of our life.

I cannot miss surely this splendid opportunity to express my special gratitude to Authorhouse team to have encouraged and accompanied me in publishing this book. Special thanks go to Erin Cohen, Senior Publishing Consultant to have tactfully pulled me on the way toward realizing my dream of becoming an author.

Last but not least, I deserve whole respect to Buzela land and all its inhabitants (humans and non-humans) to have inspired me. I pay regards to my ancestors and dead who outlive peacefully in Nzini and other Bazela's dormitories which have become today unfortunately the theaters of greedy Bakata Katanga militia and Democratic Republic of Congo government military forces.

Foreword

While attempting to scratch down these lyrics, I was quite sure that I was doing it for pleasure. The more I advanced, the more ideas perspired. Definitely, I started enjoying my own emotions before the need to share with others transpired.

Still every single poem was laying disparately either on a sheet of paper or in a notebook, dated and located differently. I certainly thought that there was no connection between them. I forgot that each single piece was collected in tranquility. It was later on that I decided to put them together in a collection even though I could not realize it was already virtual collection. I would like humbly to confess that it was not a comprehensive exercise to re-arrange metaphorical and metaphysical intertexts bearing the same idea.

As I enjoyed re-reading the text at sunset, I had been impressed by the consistence of some utterances: the reoccurrence of names (of animals, persons, birds, places...), adjectives, adverbs... At the same time, I realized that the text was inhabited by figurative languages, including but not limited to metaphors, irony, understatement, overstatement, puns, satire, aphorism, oxymoron...

Most importantly, I noticed that the collection has not only re-created the world and recalled my childhood, but also and especially it questions human's nature, his/her past and present, and foresees the future. However, the text does not spare human to savor his/her delightful experience and technological progress. And it exposes him/her to the absurdity of his/her life while denouncing his/her anthropocentrism toward nature.

In this respect, human is perceived on cross-roads, inquiring the sense of his/her existence. As a "co-creator", s/he is enjoying his/her technological progress which, however vague, is poisoning him/her either by isolating him/her from the nature and the community where s/he had been part, or by transforming him/her as cannibal. As religious, human is discovering his/her own imperfection that s/he can only overcome thanks to an awesome being above him/her.

Though the collection ends by a poem praising utopia, it does however invite human to grasp the present moment to question his/her constructed "superior" nature, the past and the present, and to act for the better today and tomorrow. This is the quintessence of the master poem which dictates the title of the collection.

Facing all above mentioned aspects throughout the collection, I honestly assumed irrelevant to refrain from sharing these insightful experience and emotions with others. Hopefully, as my readers, you will enjoy this poetry of fortification.

Mwepu Kalenga

I. Literary Zeal

0.1. I am sorry, I am Young

I am sorry, I am young
When all things in my mind thread
As pieces of tiny bread
With any threatening bung.

I am sorry when slavishly   5
Elephants crash innocent crops
That the farmer drops
Not unwillingly but spontaneously.

I am sorry to see them wandering,
Ignoring their move   10
That they search to prove
When they are fancy pondering.

I am young, I am sorry
To hear them complaining
Each single morning   15
About their salvation worry.

I am sorry, they do not comprehend
The truth they regard as nothing,
But without which they will not do anything
They tend to apprehend.   20

Through ill-sighted eyes,
Shortened whereby modern glasses,
Matched with their necklaces,
They disregard it as rotten maize.

I cannot understand, I am young,   25
The danger scandalizing Africa,
Known all over Asia, Europe and America,
Revealed through their slung.

I intrigue it through this monody
"Brush aside their past   30
And rein them last;
They will think in parody".

I am sorry, I am young
To be understood
Where I have up-stood   35
Even though within their hearts it has rung.

One day Soyinka I dreamt
In his prisoner's robe in front of a magistrate.
My spirit forward went to join him;
My soul went off beam.
Frozen I stood as a doom;   5
That day was a day doom.

I dreamt him on the stage,
Performing one of his plays strange.
Awoke, I felt attracted by his vivid performance,
Strange I was but among the audience;   10
Reluctant my spirit was,
Attracted my soul was.

Once I dreamt him at the table
Painting his melodramatic fable,
I was carried in heaven by literary angels;   15
A feather entered my metaphysical angles,
Came out with a literary band;
I awoke with a feather in my hand.

In a trail I hiked;
My soul joyfully soaked,
Yielding pith whole over my body.
While my spirit was in sublime,
My feet were no longer hasty.   5

In that reclusive world
I heard through the howling storm
A voice dictating me emotional verses.
In the sublime my spirit grasped;
I put them down; they were free.   10

Then, I realized I was a poet
And thought of Carl Sandburg,
Amy Lowell, Edgar Lee Masters
T.S. Eliot…
Who, through free verses, marked their names.   15

The more I advanced,
The more poetic I felt.
Ideas perspired,
And my soul emotionally soaked and relaxed at once
Disclosing the most hidden of myself.   20

Worried I decided one day to hike.
Leftward spread Kapanda river
Smoothly pouring downwards;
My feet made forwards.
Isolated the acre was;   05
So was the despairing spirit
Wandering in sterile verdant
Where the desire too long
Was but a river.

A cuckoo announcing darkness   10
Threatened my mind,
Awoke my emotion
When the sunset assimilated me.
Defeated, I started shuddering
In the solitary area;   15
Despair smelt
Where determination escaped.

Ceaselessly I attempted
To navigate the empty heaven
Inhabited by cloudy ideas   20
Filling my head
Before being put down…

Trembling, I scratched the first morpheme
Following a grapheme
Up to a lexis;   25
It was an emotional kennel.

The sunset set my fear,
Rose my feather
To overcome the infinite
Whereby sublime swear.   30

Why are you shy, nightingale?
Whereas you are a bird eagle.
Your genius awakens the country,
And your experience forsakes pedantry.

Nightingale, far from a pedant,   5
You are but independent.
Get in your innermost
And express the best
To set the left
Of your gift   10
That God
Has offered you as gold.

You are a bird among birds
Notwithstanding your diminutive wings.
You are petite with angelic voice,
The source of your choice.   15

Won't you praise Lord
For he has loaded
You with a golden talent
To yield but gallant
Songs of praise   20
That should raise
Poetic sensations
As if in plantations?

Do mark your name
Through your songs' fame   25
Which raises man's worry

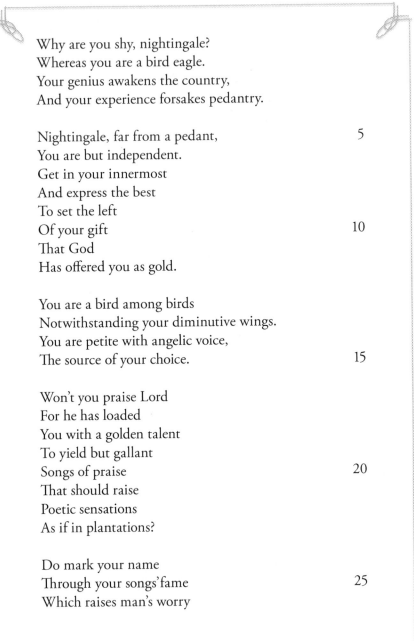

Once being sorry,
Which elevates life
While being in life,
Which praises death   30
Once being about death.

Never mark your name
Through one's wick fame.
Being alive,
Please believe   35
In the Almighty God,
The owner of that gold.
You are of the world
As the songster bird utters in a word:
Nightingale, the rose of songster birds,
Trained among girds.   40

You will inscribe your name
If you keep calm
And listen to their songs
Whose prosody and diction are boards,
Rhythm and alliteration are faces   45
That you will use as your prefaces.

The rose of songster birds,
Never be proud through your girds.
Your are a worm
Escaped from a can of worms.   50
Proud and fame will be your final rewards
After all regards.

Terrifying rose,
Once you rose
Blooming
In the morning.

You were charming   5
Though not glaring
Once tamed
Without being blamed.

You are a rose
Not as a rose   10
But a rose of prose
Which grows.

Praised are your roses
Arising feelings morose
In trembling hearts   15
Within their hats;

Raising pedantry
As if in poetry
With no formula
Whereby tabular.   20

Your roses awake neurosis
Through analysis
Without antithesis
For potential synthesis.

I've never seen
A dropping feather
With no father
Under screen.

I've never seen   5
A songster bird
Uttering a word
Which has never been.

I've never seen
Words raising pedantry   10
As if in geometry
With no sin.

I've never seen
A single handed paints
Marvelous saints   15
With no green.

I've never seen
Shallow subscripts
On his districts
As to win.   20

I've never seen
A thoughtful traveler
As a storyteller
Holding a bin.

I've never seen   25
A critic artist
Whose prosody's pist
Is decorated in green.

Your are but that hand
Far from my body.   30
Which has already
Raised my right hand.

You are but that eye
Out of my sight
Which awakened my insight   35
To a level high.

I wonder who
Samuel Coleridge
W.Word Worth's bridge
Between the two.   40

The one notwithstanding his free verses
Considers poetic diction
Not as in fiction
Where are no verses.

Though there are no meters nor feet,   45
Your scripts reflect romanticism
Through naturalistic symbolism
Inhabiting your sheet?

Once glanced at,
Confusion rises   50
To decrease
Your emotional state.

Whereas a cut insight
Reveals your side
Unobservable outside   55
Out of sight.

You are seemingly the follower
Of S. T. Eliot, Carl Sundburg, Ezra Pound…
Though you never pound
Their style flower.   60

You resemble those classic's
Whose feather dropped hot swear,
And raised fear in prayer
Once realistic.

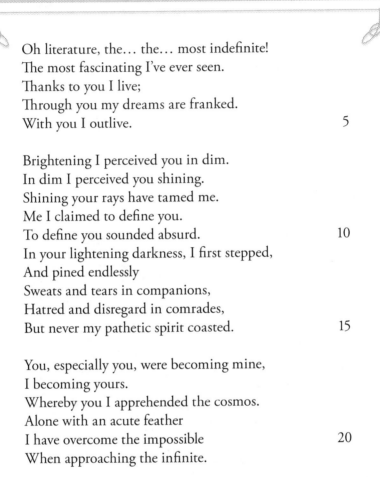

Oh literature, the… the… most indefinite!
The most fascinating I've ever seen.
Thanks to you I live;
Through you my dreams are franked.
With you I outlive.   5

Brightening I perceived you in dim.
In dim I perceived you shining.
Shining your rays have tamed me.
Me I claimed to define you.
To define you sounded absurd.   10
In your lightening darkness, I first stepped,
And pined endlessly
Sweats and tears in companions,
Hatred and disregard in comrades,
But never my pathetic spirit coasted.   15

You, especially you, were becoming mine,
I becoming yours.
Whereby you I apprehended the cosmos.
Alone with an acute feather
I have overcome the impossible   20
When approaching the infinite.

II. Natal Remembrance

0.9. My village

A glaring star
With thousand faces,
You are petite
Despite your diminutive houses,
A drawn village.   5

You, out of my memory,
Opened my eyes.
Mwepu Kenkele, the gate,
You presented me the best and the worst
Struggling unceasingly.   10
Chastening me,
You have achieved my training.

You are a natural setting;
In savanna you stand,
In-between you are: 15
Kapanda river eastward,
Lubule river northward.

Through your lens
I still perceive the world.
As a country, you have made me   20
Your eternal country man.
Your vehicle stands for my helper:
Kizela language, a stock of my past, present and future
Through which I identify
And think thoroughly   25
Before putting down enjoyable epics.

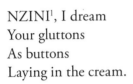

NZINI[1], I dream
Your gluttons
As buttons
Laying in the cream.

You, for years, was inhabited by my lords,   5
The setting within the water,
Stands for the shelter
Of all my loads.

You incarnated all your braves,
For your praise,   10
That deserved you a prize
Not as graves.

You are the dwelling
I have ever seen
Since I have been   15
On this stage playing.

---

[1] The Water Dormitory located in Mwepu Lwankonbe village in which Bazela Chiefs are buried.

You lighten through darkness,
Escape nightmares once in dream
With no scream.
You dim through brightness.   20

Once abandoned,
You resemble that desert
Where no concert
Is planned

Do awaken your people   25
Whose eyes shine
Against the shrine
Wandering out of principle;

Your people whose memory lost
Thus momentary   30
With no commentary,
By granting you as ghost.

What feeling not as a feeling!
It is a feeling of sorrowful dreams,
A feeling of joyful screams,
Pounding my heart,
Boiling my head,   5
Taming my soul,
Juicing my genius.

You are a warm-cold sentiment,
Awakening pedantry in solitude,
Lowering boastfulness in chorus,   10
Forsaking worry in fiction,
Revealing emotions in poetry,
Dropping fear in drama.
What a feeling out of sensations.
Whose issues destroy   15
While building,
Elevate while sinking,
Which awakens anger
Once happy.

Is it that strange move   20
Within my heart
That excites laughter in pain,
Piety in dream,
Cold in summer,
Heat in winter,   25
Nostalgia?

Or simply you are that warm voice of a dumb,
Bright eyes of a blind,
Cut ears of a deaf,
Strong legs of a lamb,   30
Or tidy breasts of a man,
Nostalgia?

Notwithstanding, I think of home
Where songster birds sing,
Where mountains and Rivers are limits,   35
Where living and dead
Are but relatives.

I think of home!
Where the blade breeze smoothly blows
Through palm wine fronds,   40
Where my heart lives,
Out of my sight
In the gallant palace.

I think of home!
Where Lubule and Kapanda rivers spread.   45
At multiple faces I dream:
The green is the "tenfuma"
The rose, "Bizungwa"
The blue "Makubwa"[2]

---

[2] All these are kinds of flowers and grasses we find in Kapanda and
Lubule rivers as well as in many rivers in The Democratic Republic
of the Congo.

I think of home!   50
Where man is never above all,
Where other cosmic beings are at ease,
Where grandfather and grandson
Are but one,
Where feast and mourning   55
Are not the same.

I think of home!
Whose remembrance raised sorrow
Whose forgetfulness awakens horror,
Whose dreams delight the soul   60
Which boils the heart.

I think of home!
Where repose the guardians,
Where my luck awaits,
Where my destiny arose,   65
Where I got "my" first glasses
Through which I perceive this world.
I think of home!
I think of home!
I think of home!   70

12. Why Africa in disaster?

Because unwillingly torn,
Because if united, then strong,
Because if peaceful then happy,
Because guarded but not guided,
Because driven from man/womanhood,   5
Because robbed altogether,
Because displayed from its lightening past,
Because thirsty and hungry,
Because gulped by blind globalization,
Because lacking the sense of independence,   10
Because used to tending,
Because uprooted,
Because desponded,
Because no longer Africa,
It is in disaster.   15

13. The Weeping Woman

Weeping woman,
Why aren't your eyes dry?
Unceasingly I heard you weeping
During the "First World War" when your brave
Men, women and children fought the strangers' war   5
To defy the unknown masters' enemy.

Again I heard you wailing
During the "Second World-War"
Once your mamma commenced
Dropping as well as your tears.   10

Once again I heard you crying
At the independence
When Lumumbas pispired
To escape you from the Tiger's nails.

Now I see you in –between   15
Fighting against neo –colonialism,
Tears collapsing endlessly
To retire your dry breasts,
No longer of the mammals,
From the Tiger's sharp nails   20
And the Lion's acute teeth.

Lonely you weep for your seeds;
Your shell snatched by those
Who freely wander you from side to side
Without any resistance   25
All your veterans in frozen beds;
Few of your warriors weakened by that weft Polio
They are continually fed.

Never mind tender mamma,
Your tears are no longer empty stream. 30
They have become poets' ink
Not used passively but actively
As acute weapon
To come up your appetite, your full liberation
That your Mandelas still hope to come. 35

14. Why are you oppressed?

Because you have accepted to be disguised,
Because you have hated your ancestors,
Because you have discarded your ways,
Because you have concurred to your division,
Because you are not men/women any more,   5
You are oppressed.

It is not that you were not strong and powerful;
Powerful you were altogether;
Altogether you withstood the oppressor;
The oppressor felt defeated;   10
Defeated he sought your source;
Your source found, he used you;
You revealed your ways;
Ways mastered, you were deprived from them;
From them you had to accept…   15
To accept heartedly his disguised religions;
His disguised religions torn your society.

Where are you my people?
Abandoned hybrids,
In – between you are   20
Seemingly thoughtful.
Wake up!
Get up!
And fight against on rushing imperialism.

If all over your corners
Are striking guns heard;
Over there fatal bombs howling.

You, for years
Were but severed naturally.   5
Mountains, forests, deserts,
Rivers, lakes, seas...
Were your bounds.

You are a worthy land at multiplex faces.
Northward lays the unbelievable Sahara   10
Coiled by the inexhaustible Nile River;
In the center spreads the Central Basin
With the marvelous Congo River;
Southward the Kalahari
With the fascinating Orange river.   15

You, for years
Saw growing humanism over individualism.
You are a land
Where from ancestors through wisdom
To youngsters poured the living water,   20
The natural land where
The Lord was acquainted whereby ancestors and spirits,
Where people joyfully
And painfully lived together with non-humans.

You, for years   25
Ignored discrimination:
Grandparents, parents, uncles, aunts,
Cousins, brothers, sisters, children
And grand children were but a whole.

Kamet of my ancestors,   30
Kamet of my grandfather,
Kamet of my generation!

You are not anymore;
You resemble that jungle
Where Tiger and Lion   35
Gain life cunningly.

You, once clandestinely torn,
Never been at ease.
You are boiling,
Boiling I saw you during the First World War,   40
Boiling I saw you at the climax
When your nationalists shrived
To save you from the Tiger's nails.

Kamet of Lumumba,
Kamet of Jomo Kenyata,   45
Kamet of Mandela,

Boiling last but not least
I see you in-between
The Tiger pulling you Westwards,
The Lion eastwards.   50

Too boiling is my heart
Wondering whether you will altogether be torn
Or released.
But who will save you
From the Lion's acute teeth   55
And the Tiger's edged nails
If your saviors worn out,
You youth hence?

Do awaken your dead youth
Though globally wicked,   60
Deprived from their ways
Dazzled through light.

I beg you, oh, Africa!
To regenerate your fascinating strength,
That power the first man gained,   65
The power from which the Kwame Nkrumahs arose;
Altogether we will stand
And struggle for your rebirth.

Where are you eagle youth?
Ignoring the truth,
Praising the tiny
For a penny.

You resemble that slave   5
Though brave
Who denied release
Never at ease.

During the 60ˢ Achebe awoke
Through his work   10
His youth
Whereby the truth.

But you still still
As if in a hill
Wherein illnesses   15
Are but weaknesses.

Is it that long way
Foreseen in Achebe's play,
Undergone by his disciples
That you grant as principles?   20

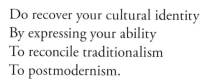

Do recover your cultural identity
By expressing your ability
To reconcile traditionalism
To postmodernism.

Save your Africa   25
From South –Africa
Through Congo
To Togo.
The strength will be poured,
Though uncoloured,   30
That the Jomo Kenyattas received
Before they perceived
That danger blaming
But not building
Africa at the keen glance.   35

Self-confidence, unity and tolerance,
Liberty and justice,
Democracy
And legacy
Will establish your Kamet   40
On which depends whole the planet.
Your past and present's regard
Will sound your final reward.

17. Let us stand and fight.

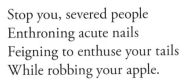

Stop you, severed people
Enthroning acute nails
Feigning to enthuse your tails
While robbing your apple.

Time has come to stand on the beam   5
And fight against imperialism
As to defend your humanism
You allude to as if in dream.

Stop, fever warrior
Whose warranty defies your youth   10
To reveal the truth.
And you stand as a barrier.

Stop, sleeping fighter
Enjoying enticing speeches
That preaches   15
Forth coming ill-liberation later.

Wake up, stand up and fight
For *Your Strong Breed*
That you never read
Even through light.   20

Why couldn't you grasp the quintessence
Of Jomo, Mandela, Kwame, Mugabe,
Lumumba's struggle?
You never ponder but giggle
Fénon, Mudimbe, Soyinka, Césaire, Senghor's essence.

Stop you, wandering seller 25
Despoiling your people's ways
Whose despondency always
Threatens despaired traveler.

You delay democracy
All over Africa wherein its basis hunger 30
With whole his youth in anger
To captivate their liberty in fallacy.

Why such a vain struggle?
It is because out of your skin
That you look of as a sin 35
When you giggle.

Look at your past
To defy your destitution
You use as your institution
To rescue your destiny last. 40

Your last destiny will be recovered
Once your powerful skin re-found
You will utilize as your own pound
And they will be bored.

All over your corners will shake 45
The strength the first man gained
Any vampire will wonder about the Paradise regained
Rather than lost, we, poets need to brake.
Let us stand up and fight all together
Against the danger spoiling Africa 50
From Egypt to South – Africa
And we will eradicate it altogether.

III. Love

18. Where do you come?

Where do you come moving love,
Launching children hearts,
Shaking youth's minds,
Holding elder's Self?

Early you knock at babies'gates,   5
Discriminating their sexes,
Opposing the likes,
Unifying the opposites
Whose screaming and laughter,
Are their sublime.   10

Your mysterious strength awakens sleeping dogs
To grasp the gist
Stirring their souls
No longer in rest
As all the rest.   15

Mathematically you approach
The weak to the powerful,
The handsome to the ugly,
The virtuous to the wicked,
The poor to the rich,   20
Why not the contrary?

Is it because you are strong,
The source of nothing and everything at once;
The Alpha and Omega,
The Omnipresent and Omniscient?   25

Thanks to your Love,
The Love within and with the Love,
I apprehend the sublime
I've ever set in utopia.

Your majesty and honor   30
Be praised!
You are the provider of that kitting love
Tying wiggler hips,
Pumping hearts within breasts,
Tenderly tongues,   35
And short – sighted eyes.

19. Awaiting love

You, my tender love,
You, the love I dreamt,
You, for years I awaited,
You, unwillingly I hoped.

Remember, one day   5
I heard your voice
Screaming and murmuring
When knocking my heart,
Though already an open door.

My stirring heart fired my wit;   10
I perceived you
Whereby my metaphysical insight,
Lightening and darkening at once.

I escaped that stir.
My heart pounding in stitch,   15
No longer a stand,
I heard a stammered voice
Yielding prompt songs,
The songs of love
Arising laughter, forsaking horror.   20

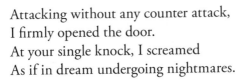

Attacking without any counter attack,
I firmly opened the door.
At your single knock, I screamed
As if in dream undergoing nightmares.

Awoke, the door was my heart,   25
The voice, my appeal;
The scream, the inflation;
Your face, the animus;
Lightening and dimming insight, my shadows,
Laughter, my totality   30

I am at ease
Though not easy
To reconcile
Animus and anima,
Light and darkness,   35
In and out,
Up and down.

20. Your eyes I love

Your eyes I love;
I truly love your breath.
Your breath shaking the breasts,
The breasts warmly I watch.
I watch through ill-sweetened eyes,   5
Eyes with illusory lens.

Your eyes I love;
I love the suited voice,
The voice murmuring my ears,
Ears with metaphysical emotive.   10
Emotive lowering and shouting at once,
At once I faint in your arms,
Your arms smoothly taming.

Your eyes I love,
I love your smiling voice,   15
The voice spoiling giddiness.
Giddiness forsook pedantry,
Pedantry raising disgust,
Disgust feelings, destroyer,
Destroyer of my lightening life.   20

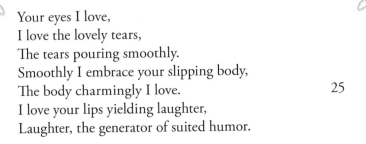

Your eyes I love,
I love the lovely tears,
The tears pouring smoothly.
Smoothly I embrace your slipping body,
The body charmingly I love. 25
I love your lips yielding laughter,
Laughter, the generator of suited humor.

Your eyes I love,
I love your hip.
The hip you wiggled. 30
You wiggled that night.
The night I reposed among the angels,
The angels of Lord
Who is himself the Great Love.

21. The ripe apple

Seemingly strange, she woke up;
I felt strange as well.
Sorrowfully she looked at me fixedly.
Her black – white eyes captured my shadow;
Her smart lips shivered.   5
Affected was my heart,
Spoilt my spirit.

Promptly I wondered why sorry
But she appeared.
She woke up all of a sudden;   10
Her lips laughingly quaked.
The cool – warm breeze interred my soul;
I felt not having felt it.

22. Remembering

Your heart flew
When the breeze blew,
The moon shone,
And my heart was gone.

You murmured between your teeth,
Stopped my breath,   5
And my heart in slow
As if in blow.

I remember I was lost
Not as a ghost.
In your calmness   10
I was breathless.

I remember, I felt in heaven
Among the seven,
All holy
I approached only.   15

And I remember, you were still
Though in drill
Where one acts
And interacts.

Your eyes appear sexual   25
As usual.
I was sexually satisfied
Without being simplified.

I remember, you came back
As soon as I took your back   30
That excited me the most
A way of my post.

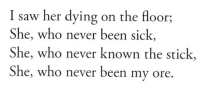

23. I say her dying

I saw her dying on the floor;
She, who never been sick,
She, who never known the stick,
She, who never been my ore.

Yes! I saw her dying on the floor   5
Where she had no memory,
Where she seemed momentary,
Where eyes became an open door.

No! I saw her dying on the floor
Till my spirit lost,   10
Till she became ghost,
And my soul a boor.

Yes! I saw her dying on the floor
Still she became still,
Still my heart in life still,   15
Still my life was but a gore.

24. The lovely letter

Here are my words,
Tampering your ears
As in those worlds
With no bears.

I utter without utterance;   5
You hear without ears
Although through an entrance,
Full of beers;
The words which lovely hurt,
And painfully tame   10
Within a heart,
Emerged in shame.

I feel them creeping,
Exciting joy and anger
Whereby weeping   15
Throughout hunger.

The ripe apple, darkening
My complexion in brightness,
Sorrow in mourning,
Worry in anxiety,   20
Love in dream.

You are an apple I dream
Whole the night with no pause,
An apple not as an apple,
But an apple I dropped.   25
When climbing up a huge tree.

Remember I slipped.
Challenged, my equilibrium lost.
Unwillingly you escaped,
Not smoothly but promptly.   30

Why couldn't you escape
That law of falling bodies
As to be suspended?
Natural victim!
Unceasingly I attempted to prong you   35
Notwithstanding the long prong like stick,
But in vain.

Once I remember you,
Sorrel apple,
Sore is my soul,   40
Ignoble my spirit,
Disgust my body.

Sore is my heart,
Pounding in stick
As I saw you dropping.   45
Slight is that love dropping in.

25. The wiggling hip

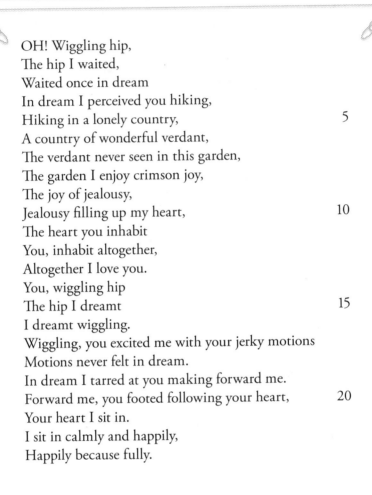

OH! Wiggling hip,
The hip I waited,
Waited once in dream
In dream I perceived you hiking,
Hiking in a lonely country,   5
A country of wonderful verdant,
The verdant never seen in this garden,
The garden I enjoy crimson joy,
The joy of jealousy,
Jealousy filling up my heart,   10
The heart you inhabit
You, inhabit altogether,
Altogether I love you.
You, wiggling hip
The hip I dreamt   15
I dreamt wiggling.
Wiggling, you excited me with your jerky motions
Motions never felt in dream.
In dream I tarred at you making forward me.
Forward me, you footed following your heart,   20
Your heart I sit in.
I sit in calmly and happily,
Happily because fully.

26. You are my rose.

You are my rose
A tender rose I sowed,
Transplanted and cared;
A tender rose whose roses
I picked and enjoyed.   5

You are my rose
Not as a rose
But a rose of wit,
A rose of love
A rose of sleep,   10
A rose of laughter
A rose of prayer.

Your entrance threatened my conceit,
Turned my heart,
Forsook worry and disgust,   15
Opened my eyes and ears
To perceive the needle-eye
And hear the voice of a dumb.

You inhabit my heart
As would the Lamb   20
Whose love alters
One's life once in belief.

Is your laughter that love
Whose blood feeds and saves,
Which feeds with love, obedience   25
Faithfulness and tolerance,
Which saves the mankind
Desperately fancying
To comprehend the apprehensible?

Your tender is above colors   30
Though yellow, my rose
You delight black, red, brown, white…
Aren't you the rose of my dream?
A rose of my endless happiness
A rose of my enthusiastic tender   35
A rose of my…
A rose of …
A…
…!!!

27. Jealousy

You resemble that mother
Whose unique child is love
She jealously loves
For his uniqueness.

The child she unwillingly waited   5
That nature clandestinely handed her
As a solely gift,
Certain and fair indeed.

Jealousy,
You equate that Gold   10
The Providence dropped
The poor picked up
And jealously kept

In that lovely pillow
Providing him the night repose,   15
Forsaking nightmares;
That he sowed in his heart,
Then felt at ease
Because cured from madness.

You are that admirable pillow   20
He can not comprehend
Cause above his head but within his heart;
That no sleep without,
Not ease away,
No dream aside,   25
Worry within.

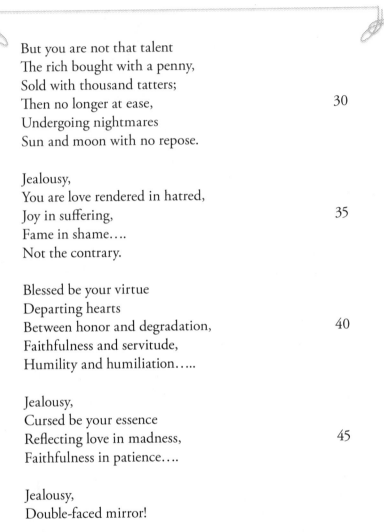

But you are not that talent
The rich bought with a penny,
Sold with thousand tatters;
Then no longer at ease,   30
Undergoing nightmares
Sun and moon with no repose.

Jealousy,
You are love rendered in hatred,
Joy in suffering,   35
Fame in shame….
Not the contrary.

Blessed be your virtue
Departing hearts
Between honor and degradation,   40
Faithfulness and servitude,
Humility and humiliation…..

Jealousy,
Cursed be your essence
Reflecting love in madness,   45
Faithfulness in patience….

Jealousy,
Double-faced mirror!

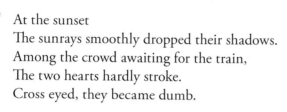

28. Departure

At the sunset
The sunrays smoothly dropped their shadows.
Among the crowd awaiting for the train,
The two hearts hardly stroke.
Cross eyed, they became dumb.   5

Sneering lips enlightened the move;
The departing move no longer a move
Joy-painful remembrance:
Joyful the past seemed'
Painful the future sounded.   10

It was a journey raising fear,
A journey carrying worry
A journey growing love
Under jealousy's humus.

It was not a journey   15
But a journey masking love in anger,
A journey disguising anger in lover,
A journey severing a heart in only one.

It goes on the railway
Transporting a half heart   20
No longer a man;
Complete she might be in dream.

It was an aching departure
Rendering 3000 miles in end of the earth,
Seven months a century,   25
A dream a death.

It was an aching departure,
Weighing love
Whereby tolerance and patience,
Faithfulness and obedience,   30
Sympathy and confidence,
Determination and faith.

29. Never mind

Never mind sweet man
Though not present
In body,
I am pleasant

Still my mind   5
Endlessly thinks
As if to bind
All things

That threaten your heart
Once awoke,   10
Ignoring why it hurt
During that work.

You dream
My love toward you
As if a simple beam   15
In desperate due,

But I am your star
Lonely awaited, never seen
At which you stare
As at screen.   20

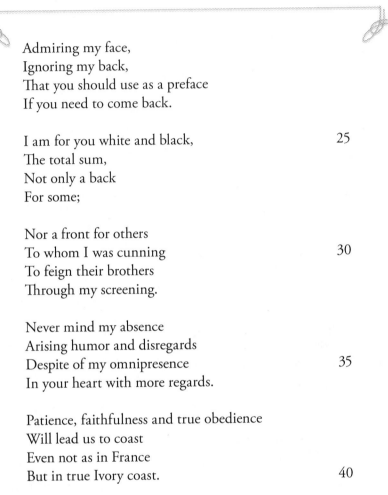

Admiring my face,
Ignoring my back,
That you should use as a preface
If you need to come back.

I am for you white and black,   25
The total sum,
Not only a back
For some;

Nor a front for others
To whom I was cunning   30
To feign their brothers
Through my screening.

Never mind my absence
Arising humor and disregards
Despite of my omnipresence   35
In your heart with more regards.

Patience, faithfulness and true obedience
Will lead us to coast
Even not as in France
But in true Ivory coast.   40

Remember that day,
The day of sorrow
When the sun sorrowfully shined,
The moon cheerfully darkened
You and I stood beside   5
Lubule river;
Looking at the sea out of our sight,
Hearing fishermen as if in play
Dealing with fishing in desert.
My heart soured   10
Ignoring the move,
Tears poured your eyes.

Remember, you asked me
If I loved you
To change your mind,   15
I told you but in hush.
You cleaned my face
With your dry cloth
Whose tears refreshed my soul
But heated my wit.   20

Remember, you told me:
"Lady, you are my everything,
And I resemble you".
I told you
That you were the sweet tomato plant
I sowed, transplanted   25
And cared with no pain
But that however vague
Bloomed sweet-sour tomatoes
That I accepted all together.

Remember, joyfully tears poured   30
When I saw you sorrowfully laughing
At the absurdity of life
That we painfully enjoy,
But Joyfully speak out.

Remember, I told you   35
Through my hush
I was but happy
Because I was you
And you were me
Though the river was the desert,   40
The Moon, the Sun
Fishes, animals
Life, death....

I prefer love;
I hate hatred.
In love we stand;
We stand all together.
In hatred we fail;   5
We fail altogether.
All together we build;
Altogether we destroy.
We build the future,
We destroy the past,   10
The future of our children,
The past of our ancestors.
Our children we love;
Our ancestors we hate.
We love them in hatred;   15
We hate them in love.
In hatred we lose them;
In love we remember them.
We lose their ways,
We remember them through children,   20
The ways of their ancestors,
The children they don't reflect.
The ancestors they should reflect in love,
They don't reflect their ways in hatred.
In hatred we have lost their ways,   25
In love we should reflect the ancestors.

IV. Death and Absurdity

32. Homage to Kyapamba

In the coffin he laid
Fixedly looking at me
With laughing lips as if in dream
Where he could awake with laughter.

Clandestinely I laughed;   5
No alive response.
I rocked, hacked out my throat
As laughing gas.
Seriously, he tarred.

From hairs to nails perspired.   10
Simple heartedly I was short tempered.
Reclusive I left, despaired my soul was;
Tears cloudily poured.

Kyapamba, a friend whose patience, gaiety,
Determination and love   15
Were his fervent comrades,
Whose brotherhood and friendship,
His weapons,
Whose tolerance and respect,
His pillows,   20
Whose suffering and degradation,
His trainers,
Separation and death
His tests.

Kyapamba, 25
You for years opened my eyes
Once in youth,
Warming my spirit towards studies,
Forsaking once for all
Solitude and stubbornness in my life, 30
Growing confidence and consideration.

Too bothering is my heart
Boundlessly boiling,
Coming out with an eternal acute question:
"Where are you from, death?
And why for? 35
For my loneliness, despair!
Though you feign of this world,
You are not at all,

You are not any more, I say.
Everything moves, but you are static 40
Centuries for centuries;
Shame, shame on you!

Just a fine line separated us,
Lightening and darkening at once.
Though my sight was hindered,
My audition grasped
The least sensitive voice.   5

Too smooth the bridge was,
I attempted but slipped;
Ceaselessly I called Kayombo over there.
No response was heard,
If not anything from the echo.   10

Further I heard, "Kwayambe[3]!"
My eyes filled with tears;
Lips full of fears shuddered.
In utopia, I was a sublime.

In the desert I painfully shouted,   15
Convinced my voice was heard,
In the world of shadows
Where response comes through dreams.

[3]   See you in God's kingdom

I waited and waited
Till the shallow breeze announced his voice   20
As if during a nightmare.
I awoke in dream,
We altogether went
Into his dwelling full of glaring household appliances,
Suitable and attractable.   25

But so quick was his move
In the rounded village
Where ancestors outlive,
Gluttons ache,
Babies and adults resemble.   30

Out of his case
I had no shelter; heavy my body was.
Escorted, I awoke:
"It was a long way but not too small".

34. Once recalling

Never mind your journey
Eternal pilgrim,
Undergone since childhood
Through youth to sunset.

Go straight to the still dormitory   5
Not to rest among
Those gluttons and brigands
Who for ages shacked the earth;

But to take repose
Among them   10
Who pause out of nightmares,
Who slip through needle eye,
Who await the doom day.

Once recalling
I perceive you crossing   15
That slipping bridge
Whose broadloom a rope
Raising fear once living.

Once recalling,
Your voice sounded a head   20
Meeting your remembrances.
Quick your moves were
In the world of shadows.

Never mind your journey,
The perpetual puritan   25
Who trips in rest,
Rests in trips.
Whose final reward
Sounds the meeting
With the lamb.   30

35. Solitude

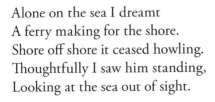

Alone on the sea I dreamt
A ferry making for the shore.
Shore off shore it ceased howling.
Thoughtfully I saw him standing,
Looking at the sea out of sight.   5

Undergoing a day dream,
He looked quite stubborn.
Strangely, he appeared virtuous
In the disturbed world.

Screams and murmurs   10
Of passengers carried him away.
Threatened his body was;
Warmed the soul was,
Cured was his spirit.

I approached his shadow,   15
And calmly stood beside.
I felt awoke when he shouted:
"I" am sorry, I was alone;
I'm sorry I was alone"

36. Still dormitory

Are you that village
Whose dormants are conscious
Of their life precious
Though with no privilege?

Are you that room within rooms   5
Resembling a plot
No longer a lot
Full of brooms?

Are you that shelter
Where Shadows repose   10
During the pause
Through a filter?

Still dormitory,
Are you still
Once still   15
As a laboratory?

Why do they ignore you
While existing
And persuading
The new?   20

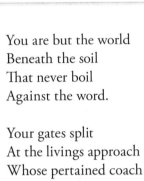

You are but the world
Beneath the soil
That never boil
Against the word.

Your gates split   25
At the livings approach
Whose pertained coach
Lit.

You are that open city
With open door   30
Under the floor
Of simplicity.

Far from open secret,
Your life probes
Even in robes   35
The concrete.

Still dormitory
Embodying living hearts,
Never shuts
Dreams premonitory.   40

37. Where do they live?

Are they in their village?
Are they in deep dream?
Are they in frozen beds?
Are they under the ground, beneath the sea?
Are they among us?   5
Such are silly and wise questions
Raised by poets.

One day I heard their voices
Screaming and murmuring
Across sliding bridge   10
Separating the two great and real villages.

I tarred at them but couldn't perceive anything
If not their feet's dew.
I hastened to join them but in vain.
My heart stitched,   15
But I felt it sounding, "sin and degradation!"

At the floating bridge I stopped
"It is great, smashing!" these are
The sneezing words dropped unwillingly.
In front opened a marvelous dwelling.   20
Wherein they footed as men.

As if in dream I was but a spirit.
I hatched the unbelievable,
The hasty world I attempted
But failed to climb up.   25
The foot –bridge separating
Brigands and angels.

Over there, they were enjoying real joy
To have fully lived on earth
Even an hour before their departure.   30
They were those who tasted the
fullness of the human life
Before entering the universe of thoughts.

Left side were those brigands,
The gluttons wandering desperately;
Whose dark homesteads surrounded   35
By sorcerers, thieves, drunkards.…

I saw the bright side
Crowded by their homonyms;
Seven babies with seven angels
Were smelling super perfume   40
Paradoxically mingled with pre–remote smoke.
It was the smoke of their ancestors
They enjoyed all together with.

Where I stood I wondered
Whether they were alive   45
Because their smoky home
Smelt the past: great, great of the greatest,
Grandfather was acquainted by his last grandson,
To the extent even to be linked to him.

As a dreamer awaked I couldn't catch the gist;   50
Only shadows marched in front of me.
Ahead I felt confident,
Despair escaped from the innermost
That sounded "They are alive,
Not of the physical world   55
But of thoughts
Where no barrier is built
Despite the fine line
Separating the winners from the losers
That cannot be transgressed once thought,   60
That man is called upon
To overcome beforehand,
To live fully before the departure
Through Self –search."

They are acute to humans' weeps,   65
To secure those who regard them as guardians,
"Yambe"[4]'s saviours.
Their home equates one's Self
That one is called to visit
Through circumbulatory process.   70

My soul came out with a woof:
"Whoever has not searched his soul
Has not yet lived"

---

[4]   Almighty God in Kizela, one of Bantu languages spoken by Bazela
      ethnic in Mitwaba and Pweto territories, Katanga Province,
      Democratic Republic of The Congo.

38. Why does a baby cry?

Why does a baby cry?
It is such an infant
But not one –sided question
That a psychologist, philosopher, psychoanalyst
And a poet raises.   5

"He cries because it is painful
To open eyes,
To hear loud noises,
To feel hunger,
To get cold…"   10
Responded the psychologist.

"He is frightened by the life's vanity;
He is worn out of life's monotony;
He is defeated towards the permanent struggle;
He is excited by the world's helplessness;   15
He is afraid of his solitude,
He is complaining of his nothingness…."
Intimately pondered the philosopher.

Why does a baby really cry?
"He does because of his cursed blood,   20
He cries because of his natural sins"
Stigmatized the psychoanalyst.

Why does he cry?
"He cries to defy man's happiness;
He cries because he loves life;   25
He cries because he needs help;
He cries because he awes the Tarry Sky;
He cries because he knows Its magnitude,
He cries not because of his emotion
but Its magnificence…"
Entangled the poet.   30

39. It is not easy.

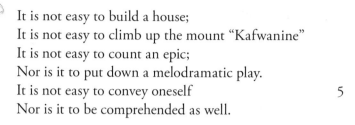

It is not easy to build a house;
It is not easy to climb up the mount "Kafwanine"
It is not easy to count an epic;
Nor is it to put down a melodramatic play.
It is not easy to convey oneself   5
Nor is it to be comprehended as well.

Living is like sailing on the sea
Where the desire is as long as the river,
Where waves stand for hindrances,
Where a canoe and a paddle are the only companions,10
Where jealousy, calumny, disregard and hatred
Are but those waves
Making forwards and backwards,
Where down and up
Are failure and success.   15

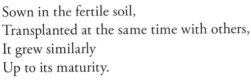

40. A Barren palm tree

Sown in the fertile soil,
Transplanted at the same time with others,
It grew similarly
Up to its maturity.

A huge palm tree   5
With heavy palm fronds,
Quite resembling others,
Seemingly fruitful,
Started blooming.

At the storm's blow   10
Its blooms collapsed.
Whole the thicket grew.
Strange it appeared;
Uneasy if felt.

Barren it was but among fertile.   15
Humiliation and disregard
Stood for its companions.
It started complaining:
"Oh! Unwilling vice, destroyer,
Disastrous and mysterious,   20
Source of my degradation,
Source of my vanity;
Shame, shame on you!"

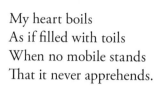

My heart boils
As if filled with toils
When no mobile stands
That it never apprehends.

My heart boils   5
Once it spoils
The innocent keen spirit
That loses its wit.

It boils when disguised
Though unpleased,   10
Ignoring their causes,
The source of its worries.

You threaten my state,
Exposing it on the plate
Where no longer at ease   15
I feel dizzy.

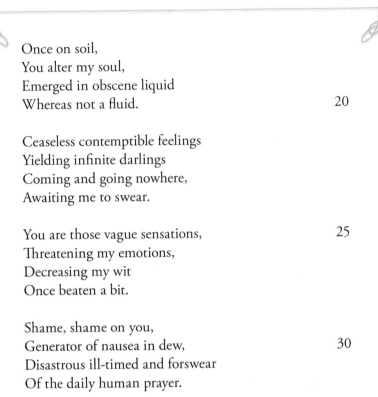

Once on soil,
You alter my soul,
Emerged in obscene liquid
Whereas not a fluid.   20

Ceaseless contemptible feelings
Yielding infinite darlings
Coming and going nowhere,
Awaiting me to swear.

You are those vague sensations,   25
Threatening my emotions,
Decreasing my wit
Once beaten a bit.

Shame, shame on you,
Generator of nausea in dew,   30
Disastrous ill-timed and forswear
Of the daily human prayer.

Who am I then
If whole is pain
Within the way
As if in play?

I am a traveler   5
With no storyteller
Whose lips slip,
Eye bows steep?

One day on a dark road
Where a lion roared,   10
I encountered a fork
Where stood a fox.

In –between lied a stump
Not as a lamb
Who saved my load   15
From abroad.
It was a stump I tried
To remove but failed
Before I slipped in vain
With much pain.   20

Threatened was my heart,
That painfully hurt
Out of pain
Because in vain.

She commenced complaining.
She, who had survived:
"Come death, come death, I'm off.
Why such a life of miseries?
Why such a life of quarrels?   5
Why such a life of dreams?"

I heard her complaining
In her smoky kitchen
Coughing and coughing
Till the cool breeze from the riverside   10
Escorted her to upland.

Delightfully, she met her mates:
"By Jove!" she screamed,
"Whole this alive!"
The natural setting   15
Reflecting the ancient one.

She couldn't enjoy it;
The quick world,
The world of shadows,
The world of spirits;   20
I remember Plato called it real instead.

Sorrowfully I heard her complaining
At her way back home.
Over there my homestead
My heart bit and wondered: 25
"She, who had outlived
Never thought about death,
Started elevating to it."
All of a sudden it stroke my heart,
And frozen my spirit.   30
Everything started floating;
I felt to vomit,
Then uttered:
"I mean nothing I am though I am."

44. Globalization

The world needs to be global
Global it pretends;
It pretends to link West to East.
West to East are hurling bombs heard.

The world needs to be global.   5
Global the Lion and Tiger shrive;
Shrive to crush innocent nails;
The nails so long overwhelmed,
Overwhelmed, live with no shelter.

The world needs to be global,   10
Global they craftily despise it.
It feels tamed whereas idle;
Idle it appears despoil.
Despoil, because it is disheartened.

The world needs to be global,   15
Global individualism primes over humanism.
Humanism is disguised in capitalism.
Chauvinistic capitalism demolishes humankind.
Humankind becomes desecrated.
Desecrated, there is no alive globalization.   20

The world needs to be global,
Global apart from human;
Human, ill –treated, becomes warrant.
Warrant is his mind wondering its leitmotiv;
Its true leitmotiv is that missing union,   25
The union with other natural forces.

The world needs to be global.
Global will it be with the godly human?
Godly human enthralling others' life and existence,
Life and existence that earth needs for its survival.   30

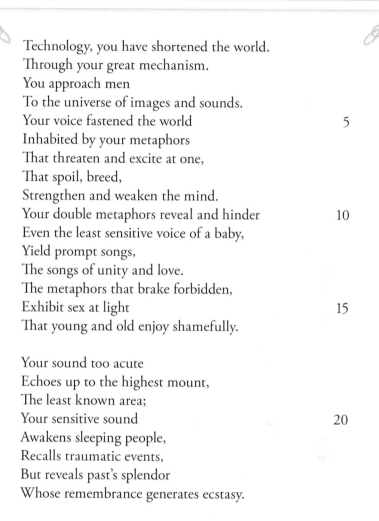

Technology, you have shortened the world.
Through your great mechanism.
You approach men
To the universe of images and sounds.
Your voice fastened the world   5
Inhabited by your metaphors
That threaten and excite at one,
That spoil, breed,
Strengthen and weaken the mind.
Your double metaphors reveal and hinder   10
Even the least sensitive voice of a baby,
Yield prompt songs,
The songs of unity and love.
The metaphors that brake forbidden,
Exhibit sex at light   15
That young and old enjoy shamefully.

Your sound too acute
Echoes up to the highest mount,
The least known area;
Your sensitive sound   20
Awakens sleeping people,
Recalls traumatic events,
But reveals past's splendor
Whose remembrance generates ecstasy.

Your shrewd sound   25
Facilitates vampires,
Elevates brigands,
Grows lies.
Your sound
Unifies people,   30
Grows love,
Sows sympathy,
Praises Lord.

Listen, aren't you half-man?
Half because you grow death   35
While preventing it;
You set sicknesses
While curing them;
You threaten man
While training him.   40
You dehumanize him
In the name of humanization.
Technology, you claim
To help man,
Not to became human, cosmic   45
But isolated,
A man whose mind is torn
Between his essence and end
That he can no longer apprehend
To come up his hunger   50
Whose final reward
Would be his Self.

46. It is a long way.

I was on the way
As I heard straightaway
A howling scream
As if in dream.

My luggage on the back   5
As an old woman back
From a further field
For a night repose with no shield.

Left side the old forest stood,
Rightward the savanna spread;   10
Over there elephants roared,
And I was bored.

In - between I was frightened.
From nails to hairs trembled;
Despair smelt   15
Where hope escaped.

Through darkness I perceived it
Making at once forward and backward that night.
Forward it attempted,
Backward the storm moved.   20

It was a vessel with no head
Where people enjoyed only beer and bread,
Feigning their pain
As if in vain.

47. When the cease fire?

The world is small
But too small is my heart
That cannot stand as a wall
To burst and hurt.

The world is global   5
And man is a vain globe –trotter,
Unfortunately the most cannibal
Of his unceasing slaughter.

In his conquest, he enthralls nature and himself
With sophisticated bombs   10
Crushing his Self
As rumbling hairs from combs.

Sailing within my heart, I heard it wondering
"When the cease fire?"
Meanwhile its voice sounded lowering   15
As entangled by my own tie.

I hope it will come
When fleshes become red,
Whole discriminations overcome,
And man and nature no longer tiny bread.   20

I hope it will come one day
When East and West will freeze
On a given Saturday
Through the breeze.
Then the scratched Africa   25
Will recover from its madness.
From Egypt to South-Africa
Will reign calmness.

48. Internet, you threaten the world.

You threaten the world
With your hasty speed
Never hindered even by the unbelievable distance
Departing senders to readers.

You escape monotony   5
Whereby your monotone diversities
Tending to extrapolate
Man's mind, you builder.

You transgress your limits
Thanks to your extravagant ambition   10
To master your master,
No longer a conductor, but a conducer.

Internet, you threaten the world
That you strengthen
Through their open relationships   15
All over the world.

Nonetheless, why do you spread
Lies imbricately but truth harshly
To the extent of being equated
To the former?   20

Why do you open the way to hell
For those ill –organizations
Robbing sleeper –awaked?
Whereas your magnificence
Would reflect positivism   25
Even though you are not of August Comte's era,
Nor sophists' epoch
To be regarded skeptically by Socrates.

Dim morning,
The morning of election,
The morning of joy and cry,
The morning of illegitimacy and fallacy,
The morning of injustice and dictatorship,
The morning of ill-sweetened laughter,   5

You grow within their hearts,
You praise the tiny for a penny.
You embellish morgues and vivify moribund
You demolish living hearts
Whose emergency threatens them.   10

Dim, you are!
The morning drying its glories,
The morning dimming its own star,
The morning-star dazzling the sunrise.

A critic eye can wonder if it will rise   15
While displayed in advance.
Perhaps no if still jacked by those gluttons
Whose sharp teeth are those of the Lion
And nails the ones of the Tiger
Threatening of sunrays to itinerate.   20
Will those isthmus' inhabitants see it?
Perhaps yes, when monarchy collapses
Not instantly but darkly,
When the isthmus becomes moldy   25
They would use as democracy's basis
To veer the vampire's hunger
From their own appetite
Because selfish
And alienated.   30

50. Time has gone

Time has gone!
It has with whole my strength;
Carrying my teeth and ears
Without leaving any hairs and nails
But generating two eyes and a leg.   5

Time has gone!
For ever it has
Without leaving any thing
If not disregard because old.
Whole wit confuted,   10
Fear and indifference prevail on tender.

Time has gone!
For sure it has hastily,
The time of my time,
The time of songster birds,   15
The time of hunters `songs,
The time of initiations,
The time of myth, folksongs and fairy tales,
The time of pantomimes, riddles and proverbs,
The time of the evening fire.   20

It has gone!
The time of rain,
The time of drought,
The time of wild animals,
The time of virgin forest,
The time of pure water,
The time of brotherhood.   25

Oh no! Time has gone
Carrying the manhood,
Spoiling brotherhood,
Praising individualism,
Forsaking humanism   30

Yes, it has gone!
For ever it has
It
Has
For
Ever!!!   30

Man is ill;
He remains still
In the solely bed
Covered by his red.

He continually ponders on his essence,   5
Encounters the Omnipresence
Who shakes his being
As a human being.

He wonders the why of his existence
In the world of quick presence   10
Where flies wander wonderfully,
And Cock-roaches enjoy blood warmly.

He is ill
Still in hill
Wherein hope escapes,   15
Despair drops.

He is ill because young
To comprehend that it has rung
To awaken his genius,
Resembling Phoebus.   20

Once he elevates to him,
He grows with no whim
Refraining him from recovering
From madness tearing
His mind   25
That he will never mind
Because cured
After being secured
By the Lamb
With no more lam.(atations)   30
That man has expected.

52. Where does it go?

Where does it go?
A sailing vessel with no bowsprit,
Rowing boats with no oars
Where dumb rowers meddled with hands
Unknowing their destination.   5

What do they do ignoring the ship's move,
Self –centered equipage
Pretending to operate the vehicle?
Embarked on the so called ship
Sleeping passengers: 10
Illiterate and literate
Dream playing music
While enjoying cunning speeches
Once misled.

In nightmare the mechanical   15
Pretends mechanizing.
Darkness dazzling him,
Heavy and cloudy sky weighting his mind,
The conductor no longer a conducer,
Was but a sleeping dog   20
Actually ignoring his fares
But dreaming leading the choir
Robbing one another with his dummies.

Awoke, he climbed up the ship,
Turned around unquestioning people,   25
Continually he wondered where it went.
He ascended the power,
Awakening short –sighted goods
Watching out of sight,
Pondering out of mind,   30
Hoping out of heart.

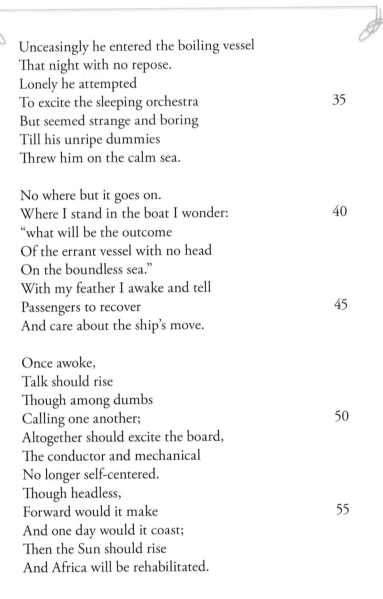

Unceasingly he entered the boiling vessel
That night with no repose.
Lonely he attempted
To excite the sleeping orchestra   35
But seemed strange and boring
Till his unripe dummies
Threw him on the calm sea.

No where but it goes on.
Where I stand in the boat I wonder: 40
"what will be the outcome
Of the errant vessel with no head
On the boundless sea."
With my feather I awake and tell
Passengers to recover   45
And care about the ship's move.

Once awoke,
Talk should rise
Though among dumbs
Calling one another;   50
Altogether should excite the board,
The conductor and mechanical
No longer self-centered.
Though headless,
Forward would it make   55
And one day would it coast;
Then the Sun should rise
And Africa will be rehabilitated.

53. A cell has made him man.

A cell has made him man
Th ough paradoxically he was
Undergoing blame
While unblameworthy he was.

Innocent flying bird   5
Condemned for black mail
As to impede his bread
That he gets whereby his mail.

Over hanging strike,
Raising fear once in tears,   10
Never implored him to brake
Thanks to prayers.

Blessed be that cavity
Firing his imagination,
Increasing his ability   15
Along his migration.

Never mind that isolation
Though painfully undergone
Whose final reward is your liberation,
Ultimately done.   20

You are cured
After overcoming that slipping road.
Thanks to unceasing prayers of oppressed,
Lord has loaded you his rod
That you will use even abroad
Before coming back home on board
Not as a lord
But with heavy load
To raise awareness of your sleeping youth
For a coming world other.

54. A house with no door

What is that house with eternal opening doors?
Whose house jambs are copper,
Door knob ores,
Its bores grasshoppers
Doormat diamond,   5
Door way steel;
Door yard back diamond,
Its roof is in wool steel?

Your doorkeeper is death,
Your door sill ash   10
Your doorman deaf,
Your doorstop lush!

You resemble that field
Wherein elephants, tigers and lions fight,
Crushing nails with no shield   15
During light;
Where bores storing seeds
Die of hunger
With their breeds
In anger.   20

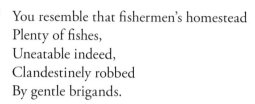

You resemble that fishermen's homestead
Plenty of fishes,
Uneatable indeed,
Clandestinely robbed
By gentle brigands.   25

You resemble my village where I grew,
But you differ from it for it belongs to its inhabitants,
You are a universal belonging
Whose destiny is decided above your head.

Before yesterday, you were a personal property;   30
Yesterday you became unknowingly a universal property.
Last week your underground attracted
you complex conflicts;
This week are your forests and rivers
That are decided upon being universal,   35
That your kids have no rightly to enjoy fully
For fear to be ejected from the unfair world order.

Time will come to close these seemingly eternal holes.
Then, sweet roses will bloom for your grandchildren.

Why do you raise her, destiny?
Is it because she was not Devine tiny,
Because she was called upon her birth
To wait for her rebirth,
Once in pain   5
Within a chain,

Or Because she has attested her way
Straight away
From the initiation
Wherein the apprehension   10
Brought her up
To sum up?

Is it because disguised, she stood
Though without being understood?
Out of sight   15
She had an insight
On her constructed nature
As if on a picture.

Is it because not through crime,
She apprehended the sublime?
Where by a word   20
She opens a world
Not as a world but toward Lord
Our eternal sword.

56. Unreachable

What is that gold,
The gold within the soul,
Never sold
As brilliant bowl?

Is it that square within the circle,　　　　　　　5
Or vice versa
That we turn as in circle
With no reversal?

Or it is that triangle made on cross-roads
That we never afford with no shelter,　　　　　10
Taking to the road?
We fall without helper to utter.

Is it simply that isolation within solitude,
Attempted through fascinating strengths,
Or just that delight never grasped in plenitude　　15
Despite the lengths?

You are divine
As you resemble the Sky
Never reached by a bine
Nor comprehended where by.　　　　　　　20

57. Patience

Patience, you are a virtue
Although you simulate suffering
In waiting for issue
Up bringing.

You are a remedy,   5
A builder at once
Though you are not ready
To rear once.

You reconcile darkness to light
Right to left,   10
Heavy to slight
With nothing left.

Under your strength, man grows.
In search of his growth,
His youth draws   15
A circle of truth
Whose issue
Is Self;
No longer true
As himself.   20

What circle do you wait?
The circle toward the circle
Still await
For oracle
To predict the outcome   25
Of the forthcoming verdict
Which will never become
An open pit.

58. It will rise

You are eternal night,
Disastrous and offensive,
Shaking up and down at once,
Dimming issues,
Shading into the shade the past   5
Whose remembrance
Though scanty scaffold!

You delay light,
Scamper scamp darkness,
The sinker of ambitious,   10
The elevator of absent –minded
And shameful hearts.

Will you end
If all cocks begs cut;
Other wise tied?   15

You delay democracy,
Dwindle peace,
Wash justice,
Browse freedom.

Heavy night,   20
Dim out and dire,
You raise dimwits,
Burden wits.

Will it rise?
One day it will   25
When the moon sets,
Heavy clouds disappear,
Bright darkening stars collapse,
The blue alters clear,
Conceited cocks awake.   30

It will rise
When the mind changes,
Nightmares cease,
Ideal speeches flew,
New heads come up   35
Through voices.

It will rise
When man becomes man;
Justice and peace
His companions,   40
Freedom and democracy
His spears,
Law's awe an arrow.

It will rise
When legacy   45
Over impunity,
Dialogue over terror,
Nationalism over tribalism
Respect over dehumanization
Bioregionalism over regionalism
Prevail.   50

A marvelous morning
The sunrays will appear
Rendering the nature natural,
The man human
Through a tender atmosphere,   55
Raising love and tolerance,
Praising totalism
In its transcendent Zeal.

59. I am happy, I am old.

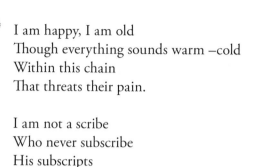

I am happy, I am old
Though everything sounds warm –cold
Within this chain
That threats their pain.

I am not a scribe   5
Who never subscribe
His subscripts
On his districts.

I am happy, I am old enough
To help them breath   10
Through these sweet-sore lines
They can regard as sneering pine

If only they are blame –worthy
Of their civilization indeed worthy
They would utilize as up life   15
Of their ancestors' gift.

I am old to fire their imagination
Through my monadic poetry, the poetry of fortification,
Stressing the forth coming man's full liberation
Whose realization   20
Never equated in circumbulatory world,
Somehow approached in shadow's world
Where they live comfortably
But unstably
Because still travelers,   25
As would count storytellers
Who assert to have visited them
Not on palm tree stem,
But through dreams
With more screams   30
That poets use as stream of consciousness
With more carefulness.

60. Time will come.

Time will come.
It will come to comprehend the mystery.
It will come to live among others
Sharing cosmic strength
Our common factor.   5

Time will come
When the Jomos will awake from frozen beds,
When the Mandelas will be reborn,
When Africa will recover its magnitude,
When Africa will bow towards its past values,   10
When Africa will reject anti-values.

Time will come
When the Sun becomes the Moon,
The Earth, the Sky,
The man, the woman   15
The up, the down
The in, the out.

Time will come,
The time of self-confidence,
The time of unity
The time of the Great tree   20
Wherein will the penguins land
And the chosen take repose,
Sharing the table with the seven.

Time will come,
The time of rest,   25
The time of true freedom,
The time of happiness,
The utopian time of the poet,
The paradisiac time of the believers
The communistic time of humanitarians   30

61. Time has come.

Time has come!
To reconcile West to East
To cleanse borders: tribal, racial
To grow love in unity
To settle the basis on rocks.   5

Time has come
To humanize nature
Not as cannibals
But humanitarians
To be part of nature for its survival.   10

Time has come,
The time of prayer
The time of tolerance
The time of self quest
The time of co-habitation   15

It has come,
The time of collectivism
The time of re-integration
The time of revival
The past time through new lens   20
The nowadays of remote centuries.

Oh, yes! It has come for ever,
The one of globalization
The one of mutual respect
The one of past regard.   25

It has come!
The time of evaluation
The time of nightingale
The time of Eagle youth
The time of wit warriors   30
The time of critics.

62. The sky will collapse.

One day it will collapse
When the lamb steps
Among the seven
No longer in heaven
Where he tares at us   5
Through tender lens
As living breed
They always breed
With lovely bread
We never thread   10
Nor throwback
To stand on back.

It will collapse
When the huge tree overlaps
Its shadow we use as shelter   15
To grow better
Our faith
Once in belief.

Will it collapse?
When everything stops   20
Sneezing breath,
Life becomes death
The Sun, the Moon;
Then none will mourn
Because no water, no land   25
But the Son will land
As the father
Among his bother.

Man will integrate
His constructed holly essence to congratulate   30
The Lord to have met the Lamb Heaven
Surrounded by all the Seven.

63. The huge Tree

The huge tree
Where songster birds repose,
Where flies and bees amuse,
Giraffe and sheep dialog,
Wherein monkeys jump.   5

Your shadow resembles that river
Crossing Eden:
Calmness, honesty, sincerity, faithfulness
Are but you.

How strange you are?   10
The beginning was you,
Paradoxically you are the end.
Before, the moving spirit was but you
Sailing on the sea.

Where are you now?   15
If among men you escaped lively
To join your seat among the seven
Where you take repose at your own right.

When do you meet them
For whom you starved for hunger and thirst   20
To appraise their blood
And saved if for ever?

Time has come to meet you
At your awesome gate,
Awaiting for just and sinners   25
No longer infused but integrated.

64. The Sublime

Climbing up the mountain,
I awe your grandeur
That you jealously maintain
Through your splendeur.

Your significance escapes any name   5
They attempt to equate in praise
As to reveal your fame
You personally appraise.

What a mercy for mankind
To be secured by the lamb   10
No longer of that kind
Of sinners whose resort lam(entations)?

You, Great Love
Who fed them with lovely breed and bread
After you died for unworthy glove   15
To save their red.

Though among them, you were but a Lord,
With your magnitude glaring.
Through your speech sword;
At you magnitude, the world was tarring.   20

God among them!
What a chance for lost
To live with the stem
Who never became a ghost.
Be praised your name,   25
The generator of whole honor
To defy the blame
They utilize as their tenor.

Who can transport me
Back into that repose world
Where saint spirits rest,
Painful bodies cursed,
Lovely soul famed;   05
Where I think I am not?

Utopia, I do admire you!
For you are but utopian
From any topic,
You resemble nothing   10
But the end of everything.

I do admire you, utopia!
At your gates, I smell liberty;
Justice and equality
Are but your gate men;   15
Your homeruns are those
Homeric laughing women.

Do I admire you, utopia
Whose house is joy,
None to employ?   20
Charity but not criminality
Is your house hold
Plenty of merciful grace
In the released palace.

Don't I, utopia, admire you?   25
In this boiling world,
I perceive through ill-sweeten eyes.
A restless world
Where I enjoy a crimson joy
As a boy,   30
Glaring poison
As in in prison.

I never admire you
For the smoking world in I live,
That I scarcely believe,   35
Which is as strange
As a burs of eggs'range.

Never do I disregard you, utopia!
Once fed of calumny, jealousy,
Disregard and hatred,   40
I metamorphose in cunning.
Satire and puns
Sum up my style
Under my disguise.

Neither do I look off you!   45
In your kingdom
I never identify anything and everything, at once
I am what I am not, and not I am.
As things do not mean:
The Moon is the Sun,   50
The Father is the Son.

In your kingdom
Where the prisoner released,
The mad recovered,
Where the fate and slender   55
Are but slim,
The rich and the poor are but alike.

Who can transport me back over there?
The shelter repose,
The monist sphere   60
Where the soul and spirit rose,
The source of poetic genius
The spontaneous world.

Why can I not admire you?
Promoted by Marx   65
As communist world,
Envisaged by Christians
As paradisiacal world,
Regarded by poets
As flowing source,   70
Granted by Thomas More In 1516.

I scarcely believe this world
Deprived of love and justice
Restrained from equality and liberty
Prevented from salvation and safety   75
Though it is but your preface.

Printed in the United States
By Bookmasters